D0929763

DATE DUE

DEC 19 '90	NOV 3 JH	
JAN 30JH	AN 1 8 Dm	
MAR 1 '91 CB	APR 3 MP	
'91	SEP 2 PR	
MAY 1 5 MP Dm		
OCT 18 '91 kz	JCB	
MAR 10 MP		
MAR 23 mP		
NW		
MAY 21 '93		
APR 2 0 TV		
MP		

Children of the World

China

For their help in the preparation of *Children of the World: China*, the editors gratefully thank Employment and Immigration Canada, Ottawa, Ont.; the US Immigration and Naturalization Service, Washington, DC; the Embassy of the People's Republic of China (US), Washington DC; the International Institute of Wisconsin, Milwaukee; the United States Department of State, Bureau of Public Affairs, Office of Public Communication, Washington, DC, for unencumbered use of material in the public domain; and Fan Yu, Milwaukee.

Library of Congress Cataloging-in-Publication Data

China.

  (Children of the world)
  Adapted and expanded from a translation of the original Japanese text.
  Bibliography: p.
  Includes index.
  Summary: Presents the life of a fifth-grade girl and her family living in Beijing, China, describing her home and school, daily activities, and the ethnic groups, religion, government, education, industry, geography, and history of her country.
  1. China—Social life and customs—1976-
Juvenile literature. 2. Children—China—Social life and customs—Juvenile literature. [1. Family life—China. 2. China—Social life and customs]
I. Miyazima, Yasuhiko, ill. II. Tolan, Sally.
III. Sherwood, Rhoda. IV. Series: Children of the world (Milwaukee, Wis.)
DS779.23.C459 1988   951.05'8   87-42576
ISBN 1-55532-207-7 (lib. bdg.)
ISBN 1-55532-232-8

North American edition first published in 1988 by

Gareth Stevens, Inc.
7317 West Green Tree Road Milwaukee, Wisconsin 53223, USA

This work was originally published in shortened form consisting of section I only. Photographs and original text copyright © 1987 by Yasuhiko Miyazima. First and originally published by Kaisei-sha Publishing Co., Ltd., Tokyo. World English rights arranged with Kaisei-sha Publishing Co., Ltd. through Japan Foreign-Rights Centre.

Typeset by Ries Graphics Ltd., Milwaukee.
Design: Laurie Bishop and Laurie Shock.
Map design: Kate Kriege.

3   4   5   6   7   8   9   92   91   90   89

Printed in the United States of America

Children of the World
China

Photography by
Yasuhiko Miyazima

Edited by
Sally Tolan &
Rhoda Sherwood

Gareth Stevens Publishing
Milwaukee

. . . a note about *Children of the World*:

The children of the world live in fishing towns, Arctic regions, and urban centers, on islands and in mountain valleys, on sheep ranches and fruit farms. This series follows one child in each country through the pattern of his or her life. Candid photographs show the children with their families, at school, at play, and in their communities. The text describes the dreams of the children and, often through their own words, tells how they see themselves and their lives.

Each book also explores events that are unique to the country in which the child lives, including festivals, religious ceremonies, and national holidays. The *Children of the World* series does more than tell about foreign countries. It introduces the children of each country and shows readers what it is like to be a child in that country.

. . . and about *China*:

Wong Chunz lives in Beijing, formerly called Peking, the capital of the People's Republic of China. An only child, she lives with her parents and attends the 5th grade of one of Beijing's better known elementary schools. Beijing is an active, progressive city, and Chunz enjoys its busy pace.

To enhance this book's value in libraries and classrooms, comprehensive reference sections include up-to-date data about China's geography, demographics, language, currency, education, culture, industry, and natural resources. *China* also features a bibliography, research topics, activity projects, and discussions of such subjects as Beijing, the country's history, political system, ethnic and religious composition, and language.

Despite Western preconceptions about the homogeneity of life in China today, the living conditions and experiences of children in the People's Republic vary tremendously according to economic, environmental, and ethnic circumstances. The reference sections help bring to life for young readers the diversity and richness of the culture and heritage of China. Of particular interest are discussions of the groups that make up the varied whole of China today, the efforts of the government to balance tradition and its communist aspirations, and the status of Hong Kong, the British colony due to become part of China proper in 1997.

CONTENTS

LIVING IN CHINA:
Wong Chunz, the Only Child

Chunz is an 11-year-old girl who lives in Beijing, the capital of China. The official name of China since the communist revolution in 1949 is The People's Republic of China. China covers 3.7 million sq miles (9.6 million sq km). This huge country is third largest in the world. Only the Soviet Union and Canada have more land. China contains over one billion people, about 25% of all the world's people.

Westerners used to call Beijing "Peking." "P-e-k-i-n-g" was the spelling that they thought was closest to the Chinese word for "Beijing." In 1979, the Chinese government set up a new system that helped Westerners pronounce Chinese names and places correctly. Now they know that the word "Beijing" sounds more like the real name of Chunz's home than "Peking" does.

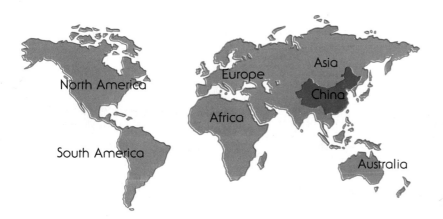

Wong Chunz and her mother (Go Yu Zin) and her father (Wong Qi Pei). Chinese wives do not take their husband's surname when they marry. Chunz's father is Mr. Wong; her mother is Mrs. Go. Children do take the father's surname; it appears first in writing.

The principal welcomes Chunz back to school.

Fifth Grade at Shi Jia Street School

When the autumn wind blows, it is time to return to school. Chunz is eager to enter 5th grade after her summer vacation, which began in mid July.

She can walk to school in five minutes, but during rush hour she often waits two or three minutes to cross the busy street near school. Bicycles crowd the street because many people commute to work on them. Few Chinese have cars.

Chunz leaves for school at 7:30 a.m.

The caretaker smiles at Chunz.

The front gate of the school.

The bulletin board with the school's rules.

Chunz's school, Shi Jia Street Elementary School, in downtown Beijing.

The 5th grade poses for a picture. Chunz is in back, fifth from the right.

Chunz's bookbag, textbooks, and school supplies.

"No wonder my bookbag seems heavy some days."

Shi Jia Street School opened in 1897. It is one of the finest schools in Beijing.

Students stand at attention for the national anthem.

The raising of the flag starts each school day.

In China, children compete to enter junior and senior high school and, later, college. Chunz studies hard so she will be ready for her exams.

Chunz was a *Sanhao* student in 3rd and 4th grades. She earned this honor by doing well in three academic subjects, gym, and conduct. Every year 15 students from each grade in the school win these awards. A student who wins one three years in a row may be allowed to compete for a spot in a highly respected high school.

The elbow stays on the desk when students answer questions.

"Do you suppose the class is always so well-behaved?"

"Today we're going to do some difficult problems in math."

Work at the computer is play for Chunz.

Chunz enjoys the programs she learns on the computer. Her school added computer classes a few years before she began grammar school. Now students can begin working with computers when they are in 4th grade.

The children's lunchbags hang on the schoolroom door.

Bowls of soup are ready for teachers to pick up.

Chunz's teacher carries the school lunch to her classroom.

After morning classes, the students are ready for lunch. Some children eat lunch at school. Others go home for lunch. In many families both parents work, but grandparents are at home to give lunch to the children. Chinese children bring their own bowls and chopsticks to school in bags that they keep in the classroom.

Chunz stays at school for lunch. She and her classmates get their bowls and chopsticks and line up in the classroom. Their teacher fills their bowls with food. Children take turns helping her. They then take their bowls to their desks and eat lunch.

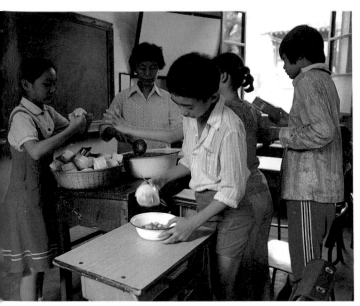

The teacher serves soup and Chunz serves *manto* (Chinese bread).

"I like meat and vegetables."

After lunch the children put their heads down on their desks and rest.

The school and playground are quiet while the children put their heads on their desks. But then the children go out to the playground to jump rope or play ball or tag.

At 1:10 p.m. the bell rings to start the afternoon classes. All the children are back in their seats for the 5th period study hall. Every day at Chunz's school, the children have a study hall so they can do their homework and be free after school for other activities.

Success in school is important to Chunz. She dreams of studying outside China and wants to be a foreign diplomat eventually. But sometimes she thinks she might like to be an actress. She has already had small parts in movies and television shows.

Sometimes the children clean up the playground when it has gotten too dirty.

The boys get set to run in a game of tag.

During the mid-day break children run and play on the playground.

This handmade ball is filled with soybeans.

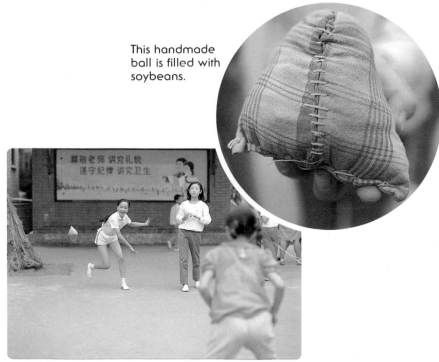

"I'm good at the broad jump!"

Chunz has quite an arm for a little girl.

Teachers' Day

Once a year, the school sets aside a day when students and parents honor teachers. The children put on a program. They practice all year so that they can perform for their parents and teachers and make them proud.

Chunz always enjoys this show. People do not wear makeup or jewelry in China, but for the ballet Chunz may use makeup so that her features will show clearly on the stage. She and her classmates have spent many hours after school so that their ballet will be beautiful.

"Aren't those three going in the wrong direction?"

Chunz is caught laughing . . .

. . . and in a serious mood.

"Do you think we've had enough practice for today?"

Activities After School

The arts have long been
important to the Chinese. China is
famous for its beautiful paintings
and sculpture. The Chinese also
love theater, ballet, and opera.
Audiences like to see players
perform traditional Chinese works
as well as works from Europe or
North America. They also enjoy
art that tells them about their
revolution.

"We make a wonderful jump-rope team."

Twice a week at Chunz's school, special teachers come from outside to
help students learn about these and other arts. The students attend
classes in Japanese, English, brush painting, oil painting, and dancing.
Chunz has taken ballet lessons for four years.

But one of her favorite activities is jumping rope. After school she meets
with the teacher who comes to coach students who want to do it well.
Schools in China compete at jumping rope. Chunz's school has taken first
place for the last few years.

When Chunz goes home after school, she continues to practice. In
her apartment building are two friends who like this sport as much
as Chunz does.

Chunz and Her Parents at Home

Chunz's family lives on the first floor of a four-storied apartment building in a busy section of Beijing. They came here from Tianjin when Chunz was five years old. Once the building was headquarters for five theatrical companies, but now 20 families live there.

It is not unusual for the Chinese to make apartments out of large buildings such as this. After the revolution, some mansions were broken up into apartments so that more people would have places to live.

Chunz and her father use a string bag to carry bottled drinks to their apartment.

"Our bathroom gets crowded in the morning."

Chunz walks through the first-floor hall.

The phone is in the hall.

The kitchen is on the first floor.

The apartments in this building are not large or fancy. Most Chinese people do not own many things privately. Instead, two or more families will share one kitchen, one bathroom, and one phone. In Chunz's building, the kitchen is outside, in an alley, and the bathroom is down the hall.

Mr. Wong, Chunz, and Mrs. Go on the bed in their small apartment.

Chunz is proud
of her artwork.

Chunz and her parents
live in one room where
they eat, sleep, read,
work, talk, and watch
television. In it are a
large bed, a chest of
drawers, a desk, a
refrigerator, and a table.

The apartment is well-organized and seems larger than it is.

Chunz is a sleepyhead, but her mother sees that she is up fairly early.

Chunz eats her breakfast of bread and milk at the desk.

Chunz's parents would like an apartment with at least one more room. But it will probably be a long time before they get it because China has a serious housing shortage. For over 10 years, the government has been building high-rise apartments so there will be more places for people to live.

Chunz has lived in this apartment since she was five. It does not seem small to her because she is used to it. Her parents arrange it carefully so everything has its place.

The Only Child of Creative People

Chunz's father, Mr. Wong, edits a magazine which is published by the Chinese Theater Company. He is also an illustrator. He has high artistic standards. Chunz's mother, Mrs. Go, works in theater also. She is in charge of costumes for a theater in Beijing.

From 1966 to 1976, China had what was called the "Great Proletarian Cultural Revolution." A group of government leaders attacked the Chinese that they thought were not following the goals of communism. Writers, teachers, and journalists were told what to say. People in the theater, symphony, opera, and ballet could perform only works that promoted the goals of communism. It was a difficult time for people who worked in the arts. Chunz's mother and father are grateful those days are past, but they are worried because Chinese leaders are again becoming strict.

After Chunz does her school work, Wong Qi Pei uses the desk so he can do some illustrations.

Chunz enjoys the moments she has with her parents.

The Chinese government controls the country's huge population by asking people to marry when they are in their mid or late 20s and by urging them to have only one child.

The biggest problem with China's increasing population is having enough food for all the people. Even though China produces a great deal of food, it must import several million tons every year. Shortages of housing and clothing also create serious problems when the population increases.

The only child appears a lot in the family album.

"See my keyboard, jewelry, and harmonica?"

Chunz's award for being a Sanhao student.

Families with just one child, like Chunz's family, are common in the city. In the rural areas, where 98% of the people live, larger families still appear. The majority of the Chinese people are Han, but some of these rural people are minority nationalities such as the Uygur, Hui, Mongols, Koreans, Manchus, Zhuangs, Miao, and Tibetans. These national groups also break the one-child rule. The government allows them to keep some other traditions, such as festivals, that their clan enjoyed before the revolution.

But rural people are even poorer than those in the cities, so they too may have to adopt the "one child only" rule in order to feed and educate everyone. Having only one child is difficult for the Chinese because family life is important to them. Children are taught to respect their parents and other adults, and children are much loved by their parents.

Calligraphy

Mr. Wong is teaching Chunz to do calligraphy, Chinese brush writing. This is a skill that requires careful and beautiful "writing" of the hundreds of characters in the Chinese written language. To the Chinese it is not just a form of writing. It is a 3,000-year-old art form.

A Chinese "character" stands for an idea. In order to read a Chinese newspaper, you would need to know 1,500-3,000 characters. In order to read an English-language newspaper, you need to know only 26 letters. These letters combine to form ideas.

Pinyin, the system using the Latin alphabet for Chinese sounds, is becoming more common in writing. This could be a mistake. People could forget how to write Chinese characters and this beautiful form of written Chinese would become a dead language, known only by scholars.

Chunz's parents are proud that Chunz wants to learn this ancient art.

Chunz's mother, in her cooking clothes, works in the building's kitchen.

Chunz sometimes helps with foods prepared in the apartment.

China's Gourmet Cooks

The kitchen fills the halls with good smells. The Chinese love tasty food — not the beef chop-suey and rice common in North America. When they can afford it, they eat noodles, dumplings, bread, eggs, fish, sea-food, chicken, duck, pork, and many varieties of vegetables and fruits.

Mrs. Go and Mr. Wong are making *baotzu*. Kneading the flour requires strong hands, so some people think this is a man's job. Women mix the filling that is put into the dough.

Baotzu is flattened dough wrapped around filling and deep fried or steamed. Sometimes Chunz helps, but often she does not make all the pieces the same size. Her mother teases her, telling her that if she helped more often she would get better at shaping them.

Mrs. Go makes beef and chives filling for the baotzu.

The family enjoys dinner in front of the television set.

29

Downtown in Beijing

Beijing has been the capital of China since the 1200s. Ming emperors built a wall around it. Later, when the Manchus ruled China, they divided it into four parts: the Tartar City, for the Manchu people; the Chinese City, for the Chinese; the Imperial City, for government; and the Forbidden City, for the emperor and his court. Now these areas are open to the public. Visitors like to walk in the courtyards, gardens, and palaces.

Chunz likes it when her parents take her to downtown Beijing.

"Here's what I would like for my New Year gift."

At least there's no pollution in a bicycle traffic jam.

China does business with some companies from capitalist countries, like Sony, from Japan.

"What would you like to see next, Chunz?"

About 9,000,000 people live in Beijing and its suburbs. The streets are crowded with people on bicycles, and the sidewalks are filled with people on foot.

The busiest places downtown are the children's stores. People jam these stores. Although families shop together, Chinese children do not ask for many presents because they know that their parents have little money to spare for gifts.

After walking for a couple of hours, the family stops at a restaurant. Some people do not go to the restaurants. They stop at food booths along the streets and buy snacks.

Feeding all the people is important to the Chinese government. About 80% of the people work in agriculture. China has less farmland than the US but must feed four times as many people, so it gives food out in fixed portions called "rations."

Rural Chinese eat simple meals of vegetables and grains such as rice, wheat, or millet. Sometimes they add pork or chicken. There is lots of hot tea. People in the cities have more variety to choose from.

"This is my favorite restaurant."

An outdoor booth where people buy cold noodles, baotzu, melon, and other nourishing things to eat.

Three-wheeled trucks are common sights on city streets.

Food booths often stay open late into the night.

A Beijing trolley goes by in a blur.

Large slabs of stone pave the straight road to Tianjin.

A Visit To Tianjin

Chunz and her parents were born in Tianjin, a city about three hours by car from Beijing. They moved to Beijing when Chunz was five years old.

Chunz and her parents like to visit relatives in Tianjin. It is time to celebrate the New Year, so they take a taxi all the way. It is an exciting trip for Chunz. At one point her father stops the taxi and runs to get some juice and cookies to have along the way. They joke and laugh as they travel, happy to be going to Tianjin.

Away from the busy main section of Tianjin is an old district with brick houses built close together. At the New Year, red ornaments hang on front doors to keep evil spirits away. Children carry animal-shaped kites and balloons. The Chinese enjoy this holiday.

Chunz and her mother walk past a large house now made into apartments.

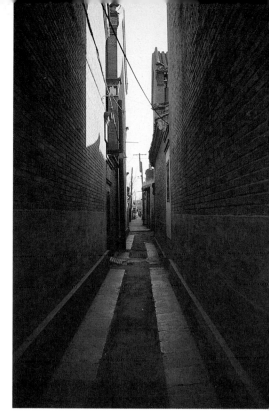

A narrow alley in Tianjin.

The winter sun shines on doorways with New Year decorations.

Residents air clothes in the courtyard.

Chunz and her parents with the Go family.

"I love chicken eggdrop soup."

"You've gotten heavier since I saw you last."

First they stop to see Mrs. Go's mother. Mrs. Go's brother, Chunz's uncle, is waiting for them. He opens the door and, with his arms open wide, he welcomes them in. Chunz is happy to see her uncle.

Mrs. Go looks around the house where she grew up and where she lived when Chunz was born. She is filled with happy memories, pleased to be with her family again. Chunz is also glad to see her relatives. But most of all she wants to see her four-year-old cousin.

Soon it is time to go to the home of Mr. Wong's parents. They are waiting with a special New Year's dinner. At the dinner table they all talk about Mr. Wong's childhood.

Chunz laughs when she hears some of the funny things her father did when he was a little boy. Mr. Wong tries to act very serious, but he finally laughs too when he remembers mischief from his childhood.

At midnight, Chunz and her parents kiss everyone goodbye and make the return trip to Beijing.

"Look over there, Chunz. A dragon got loose in the park."

"In Tien Tan Park the dragons are friendly."

"We're so wrapped up against the cold that we can hardly move."

A mother and child enjoy the winter sunshine at the New Year.

The Chinese New Year and Other Celebrations

The Chinese people use cycles of the moon to set up their calendars and holidays. For instance, New Year's Day does not fall on the same day every year, but comes anytime between mid January and mid February.

The New Year is a much-loved holiday in China. Even though it is winter, people are out in the streets and parks celebrating. They are bundled up in warm coats or jackets.

"Don't wander off, Chunz, or you might get lost."

New Year's Eve and the first three days of the New Year are national holidays in China. On the New Year, people make a new start. They pay off all debts. They add a year to their age no matter when they were born. They clean and decorate their houses, prepare special food, and wear new clothes to celebrate with family and friends.

Other holidays celebrated in China are Labor Day (May 1), Army Day (August 1), and National Day (October 1). Many of the same events and activities occurring at the New Year appear again when the Chinese celebrate other holidays. For example, there are always parades and rallies.

Banners with New Year slogans written in large Chinese characters appear along the streets and in public places. Acrobats, actors, singers, and dancers perform. There are games and athletic contests, signs and flags, lanterns and papier-mache dragons and other beasts. The day ends with dancing and fireworks.

Having fireworks on holidays is an age-old tradition. The Chinese invented gunpowder and fireworks. People used to believe that the loud noise of the New Year's fireworks would chase away the evil spirits.

Performers appear on an outdoor stage.

One man shows off his sense of balance.

Ancestor worship was once an important part of the religion and life of the Chinese. For hundreds of years, the Chinese people felt that their first loyalty was to their ancestors and their family, rather than to their country. Ancestor worship is also part of the New Year celebration, when people make offerings to their ancestors. Because the government wants loyalty to the country rather than the family, it discourages ancestor worship. But some people, especially in rural areas, still practice it.

The communist government of China does not promote the practice of religion. The communists who took power in 1949 closed places of worship and tried to get people to give up religion. They believed religion would work against the ideas of communism. But lately the government is not so strict. Now Christian churches, Muslim mosques, and Buddhist temples are open again. People may worship. But they must not try to convert others to their religion.

Cakes sell fast at an outdoor booth for sweets are uncommon in China.

At one time holidays had religious meaning to many Chinese people. Now they are times to celebrate and relax from work. The younger Chinese people have never known the meaning of holidays as their parents and grandparents did.

Two athletes in a dangerous-looking mock battle.

"I have enough money for three cookies."

"I want fireworks that sparkle rather than pop."

Crowds of people enter and leave the park.

It is New Year's Eve. Chunz, her parents, and a guest watch a special television program with music, comedy, and magic. When the program ends at midnight, Chunz dashes outside. Her father follows her, holding bamboo sticks with fireworks tied to them. Out on the street in front of the apartment, people are already shooting off their fireworks. From alley to alley, fireworks are going off. The whole town is noisy.

Chunz's father lights the fireworks on the pole. They explode one after another, almost 200 small explosions. Chunz covers her ears and grins. She knows that no evil spirits can stand such a racket. They will be frightened away. It will be a happy New Year.

Lighting the fireworks ends the celebration of the Chinese New Year.

FOR YOUR INFORMATION: China

Official name:
Chung-Hua Ren-Min Kung-Ho-Kuo
People's Republic of China

Capital:
Beijing (Peking)

History

Prehistoric China

China is believed to have the oldest living civilization in the world. Carvings on bronze vessels and turtle shells tell about China over 3,500 years ago, but people lived in China long before that. Prehistoric humans that scientists refer to as Peking Man lived from about 250,000 to 500,000 years ago in northern China. For thousands of years early humans roamed, gathering fruit and seeds and hunting for meat. Over thousands of years, they learned to make things from stone, bronze, and iron. Eventually, they began farming in northern China. Settlements grew into small cities in the lowlands. Small family groups, called clans, controlled some areas.

The Dynasties

Gradually, powerful families began to rule larger parts of northern China. A group of rulers who followed from one ancestor is called a "dynasty." China was ruled by dynasties from around 2200 BC to AD 1912. The rule of the dynasties was often upset by periods of disorder when clans fought.

Many great discoveries and achievements took place during the dynasties. These include the creation of lovely bronze vases, a writing system the Chinese still use, and the Great Wall of China. Islam appeared in China, and Buddhism increased in popularity. Other Chinese achievements included paper, porcelain, printing, gunpowder, the magnetic compass, and movable type. In general, under the dynasties China expanded its territory and the arts flourished.

The Chinese began trading with India and southwest Asia in the 3rd century AD, and by the late 13th century Marco Polo, of Venice, Italy, had traveled in China. His tales of China's wealth made Europeans eager to trade with China.

Around 1279, Mongols from Manchuria, ruled by Genghis Khan, invaded northern China. Kublai Khan, another Mongol leader, began the Yuan dynasty, which lasted from 1279 to 1368. This was the first time that all of China had been ruled by a foreign power. The Mongol rulers were gradually overthrown and driven out of China in the 1300s.

In 1644, the Manchus from Manchuria invaded China. They ruled as the Ch'ing dynasty until 1912. At first, China grew rich. In the 1800s, Western nations were running out of silver to pay their trading debts in China. So the British East India Company began smuggling opium in to exchange for tea. The Chinese, angry about opium addiction, insisted the British stop bringing opium into China. England then started the first Opium War, which lasted from 1840-42. China lost, and Hong Kong, an island on the coast of China, became a British colony. Its natural harbor made it a perfect place for European traders to do business with the Chinese, and they continued to do so, with China losing money because of the conditions created by Westerners after the Opium War. At the end of the second Opium War in the 1860s, China lost more land. England signed a 99-year lease on Hong Kong and the Kowloon area. This lease will end in 1997, and the 5,500,000 Chinese living in Hong Kong will once again be citizens of China — today, the People's Republic of China.

Modern China — Rebellion and the New Republic

The Ch'ing dynasty was troubled by rebellions in the late 1800s. A war with Japan in 1895 and European involvement in China's affairs weakened the dynasty still further. In 1905 a rebel movement began, led by a young doctor named Sun Yat-sen. In 1911, Chinese soldiers joined the rebellion. All the provinces in the south and central regions broke from the Ch'ing dynasty. With Sun Yat-sen as its first leader, China became a republic in 1912. As time went on, two groups struggled for power: the *Kuomintang*, or Nationalists, and the Communists. The Nationalist leader, Sun Yat-sen, died in 1925, and the Nationalist general, Chiang Kai-shek, took his place. By 1928 most of China was united under control of the Nationalists.

The Imperial Palace in Beijing.

In 1934, to escape the Nationalists, 100,000 Communists began the famous Long March across mountains and deserts to safety in Shensi province. Only about 20,000 survived the march.

United Against Japan

During this period, in 1931, Japan had seized Manchuria. The Nationalists were not strong enough to fight Japan while they were still battling the Communists. So the Nationalists and Communists united to fight Japan. But the Japanese had a stronger and more modern army than the Chinese. By the end of 1938 Japan occupied much of eastern China.

During World War II, China joined the Allies — France, Great Britain, the US, and the USSR — to fight against Japan and Germany. Although the war greatly weakened China, Japan surrendered in 1945 and left its Chinese territories.

China After World War II — Divided Again

By 1946, the Nationalists and Communists were at war again. The Communists won. In 1949, the leader of the Communists, Mao Zedong (called then Mao Tse-tung) set up a new government in Beijing (Peking). He made Zhou Enlai (called then Chou En-lai) the premier. The China they led became known as the People's Republic of China. Chiang Kai-shek and the Nationalists went to Taiwan, an island off the coast of China. For years, the West considered Nationalist China, or the Republic of China, on Taiwan, to be the real China. Many European nations recognized the People's Republic as the official China in the 1940s and 1950s. But until the 70s Cuba was the only nation in the Americas that recognized the People's Republic as the official China.

China Under the Communists

In its early years, the new government worked to get rid of those who opposed China's brand of communism, a system in which the government owns almost everything and gives out to people what they need. The government imprisoned or killed many people. But they also tried to improve industries, farms, housing, and health for the people. Land they took from big landlords became government property to be farmed by peasants. Industries and businesses also became government-owned.

In the years since the revolution, life for most Chinese has gotten better in some ways, but there are also problems. Sometimes the government makes mistakes. For example, during the "Great Leap Forward," from 1958-1961, everyone was to work hard and the economy would prosper. People did work hard and long, but the government had set goals that were too high. There was a lot of waste. Later, in the Cultural Revolution, the government punished those who did not support its socialist goals. Troops called Red Guards destroyed art treasures and literature, closed down the universities, silenced journalists, and tortured and imprisoned people they did not think upheld the goals of the revolution.

The relationship of the People's Republic with the outside world has not been a simple one. For decades, it has feuded with its powerful communist rival and neighbor, the Soviet Union — even as its relations with the US have warmed up during the years following the Vietnam War. Today government leaders are trying to make China more modern. They are letting people own some property, and they are trading with capitalist countries.

Population and Ethnic Groups

In 1986 China's population was about 1,076,900,000. That means about 20% of all people living on the Earth live in China. Shanghai and Beijing are huge cities, and 13 other cities have more than 1,000,000 people. Yet 79% of China's people live in small towns and rural villages.

About 94% of the people are of the Han nationality. The Han people have traditionally followed the teachings of Confucius for thousands of years.

There are 54 minor racial or ethnic groups in China with a population of about 67 million. Most live in the National Minority areas: Xinjiang, Inner Mongolia, Tibet, and Manchuria. Some of the minority nationalities are Muslims or Buddhists; others have spiritualist beliefs based on nature gods. China's leaders have allowed these people to follow some of their traditions, partly because the position of these groups along China's border is an important one. So the leaders do not want to weaken China's borders by forcing the government's ideas on the minorities and angering them.

Government

China is divided into 22 provinces or states, five minority regions, and three large cities that are directly under the central government — Beijing, Shanghai, and Tianjin.

The 1982 constitution says that China is a socialist state led by the working class and based on a union of workers and peasants. In a Chinese election, the Communist Party chooses the candidates the people may vote on. The leader of the Communist Party is more powerful than the president. China's legislative groups include the National Congress, the Central Committee, and the Politburo, which is the most powerful policy-making group in the Communist Party.

The Chinese Constitution guarantees many rights also guaranteed by the US Bill of Rights such as freedom of speech, assembly, and religion. But the Chinese people can publish or say very little that does not fit the aims of the Communist Party. The Chinese Constitution also says people have the right to work and to be supported by the government if they are old or disabled.

Language

The Chinese language is one of the oldest in the world. Although 95% of the Chinese speak this language, they speak many different dialects. These dialects have different tone systems, or pitches of sound. These tones give Chinese a musical sound. A person from one province may not understand a person from another. To correct this, the government made the Mandarin dialect standard Chinese, and now 70% of the people speak this dialect.

Chinese writing, called calligraphy, requires that people learn characters, not letters. To read a newspaper, they must know 1,500 to 3,000 of these characters. College graduates know 5,000 characters, and scholars might know 50,000. In the 1950s a committee took 800 of the most-used characters and made them more simple. These now appear in newspapers, magazines, and books, so more people can read. Another change was to write the sounds of Chinese in the 26 letters of our alphabet. This form of Chinese, called *Pinyin*, is used for Chinese names and places. The Chinese have created this for English, French, Spanish, and German works published in China.

Religion

Religion was once important to the Chinese. The major religions were Confucianism, Buddhism, and Taoism. Most Chinese believed in a combination of these three and in ancestor worship. Rural people believed in many gods.

Around 500 BC, Confucianism became popular. It is a moral philosophy more than it is a formal religion. Confucius taught the rules of good behavior and respect for superiors, elders, and ancestors. Buddhism began in India around 500 BC and came to China before AD 100. Buddhists look for peace in themselves, not in material things. They built many beautiful temples and large statues of the Buddha. Taoism preaches that everything and everyone are equally important and asks people to see themselves as part of nature.

The Great Wall of China.

About 25,000,000 people are Muslims. Islam never became important to the Han majority in China, but it is the largest minority religion.

Christian missionaries came to China in the 1500s and 1800s. The Chinese often resented and sometimes attacked Christians for bringing strange ways and for trying to stop ancestor worship.

Despite this, when the Communists took over in 1949, there were many Christian schools, universities, and hospitals.

China's leaders think religion is superstitious. They have changed some historic temples and mosques into schools, museums, or meeting places. During its early years, the new government tried to get people to give up religion. Today most places of worship are open, and the government allows people to worship. But it does not want worshippers to talk others into becoming religious.

Art and Music

Important art museums all over the world show Chinese painting, sculpture, and pottery. For centuries, the Chinese have loved the beauties of nature and of art.

Painting

Early Chinese paintings were about people or creatures such as dragons. Later, painters created beautiful art showing trees and water. They stressed harmony between humans and nature. Often Chinese writing, called calligraphy, is part of these paintings. The Chinese consider calligraphy their highest art.

Sculpture and Pottery

Pottery has been part of Chinese culture since prehistoric times. In ancient times the Chinese placed small bronze or jade sculptures in tombs. Archeologists recently found thousands of life-sized clay figures of people and horses buried near the tomb of the first emperor of China.

Music, Dance, and Drama

Chinese music sounds different from Western music for several reasons. While we have eight tones, or notes, the Chinese have five. Singers in a chorus or instruments in an orchestra all follow the melody and sing the same notes instead of harmonizing, as Western musical groups do. Today, however, many Chinese musicians know the eight-tone scale, play Western instruments, and perform traditional Western music.

Opera is China's favorite form of drama. Ballets based on the revolution show the struggles of the Chinese people that resulted in the victory of the Communists. Ballet companies can also perform traditional Chinese and even Western works as long as they do not attack the government or its ideas.

Literature

Poetry may be the oldest and most honored form of literature in China. But the Chinese also respect novels, dramas, and writings on history and morals. Since the

53

19th century, Western literature has influenced Chinese literature. After 1949, the government controlled literature. But today there is more freedom, although writers who criticize the present government may still get into trouble.

Currency

The official currency is the *Renminbi,* or RMB. The denominations of the RMB are the *yuan,* the *jiao,* and the *fen.* One yuan equals ten jiao. One jiao equals ten fen. RMB may not be taken out of China.

Agriculture

Farmers work only 20% of China's land. They do not use the valuable land in the more populated areas for pastures. They graze livestock instead in remote places like the Mongolian Plateau. To use hilly areas for growing food, they build flat terraces on which they plant crops.

About 80% of the people work in agriculture. The government has made great efforts to improve farming. They have cooperative groups, called communes, that often own the equipment that farmers use.

The climate and growing season in the south differ from that in the north, so crops differ. In the south the major crop is rice. Other crops are tea, vegetables, fruits, and mulberry leaves to feed silk worms. In the north, the principal crop is wheat. Other northern crops are soybeans, apples, peaches, and other fruits and vegetables. Cotton, tobacco, and peanuts are also important crops in China.

Industry

China needs money, so it produces goods more for export than for its own use. The most common are textiles and food products, but China also makes radios, watches, sewing machines, and bicycles.

China is one of the world's top producers of steel. It also makes machinery for new factories, fertilizer and other chemicals, trucks, tractors, train locomotives, and ships. To improve China's industry, the government is making its factories more modern with the help of foreign companies. It is sending more students abroad for training, improving its transportation system, and trying new ways to pay people so they will produce more.

Natural Resources

China has lots of fuels — coal, oil, and natural gas. In the north and northeast are many iron mines. Other metals mined in China are tin, lead, copper, tungsten, and zinc.

Rivers also provide fuel. On the banks of the larger rivers are hydroelectric plants. But forests do not provide much fuel. They cover only about 10% of China's land and are hard to reach. So wood is scarce and expensive. To meet this problem, the government is now protecting forests and planting trees. All the seas, rivers, and lakes of China have made it possible for China to become one of the leading fishing nations of the world.

Land

Only the Soviet Union and Canada have more land than China. The US is slightly smaller than China. China is full of contrasts. The highest point in China is Tibet's Sagarmatha, or Mount Everest. It is 29,028 feet (8,850 m) high and believed to be the tallest mountain in the world. The lowest point, in the northwest part of China, is 505 feet (154 m) below sea level. It is an oasis near the Takla Makan, one of the world's driest deserts. Other deserts in the northern part of China are the Ordos and Gobi. Besides deserts, China has some very wet and fertile lands along seacoasts and river valleys. The Yellow River floods so regularly and causes so much damage that it is nicknamed "China's Sorrow."

Mountains cover two-thirds of China's land. The land slopes downward from the Quinghai-Tibet Plateau, the "roof of the world," where Mount Everest and other great mountains rise. It slopes through flat areas, called basins, rises again in lower mountain ranges, and drops downward to the sea.

The long Yangtze River is in China. Only the Nile and Amazon are longer. Another long river is the Hwang Ho, or Yellow River. It gets this name because of the yellow silt it carries. Many important cities line its shores. Its valley is sometimes called "the cradle of Chinese civilization" because archeologists have found objects left there by ancient peoples.

Climate

The climate of China is as full of contrasts as its land. The southern coast of China, including Taiwan and other islands, has tropical weather. The northeastern area has severe winters. Snow covers the mountaintops of Tibet all year. In the deserts temperatures can go from a high of 100°F (38°C) to a low of -30°F (-43°C) in one day.

Most of China is in the northern temperate zone and has four seasons. In winter, monsoon winds bring cold, dry air from central Asia to much of China. In the summer they bring warm, damp air from the sea and with it much rain.

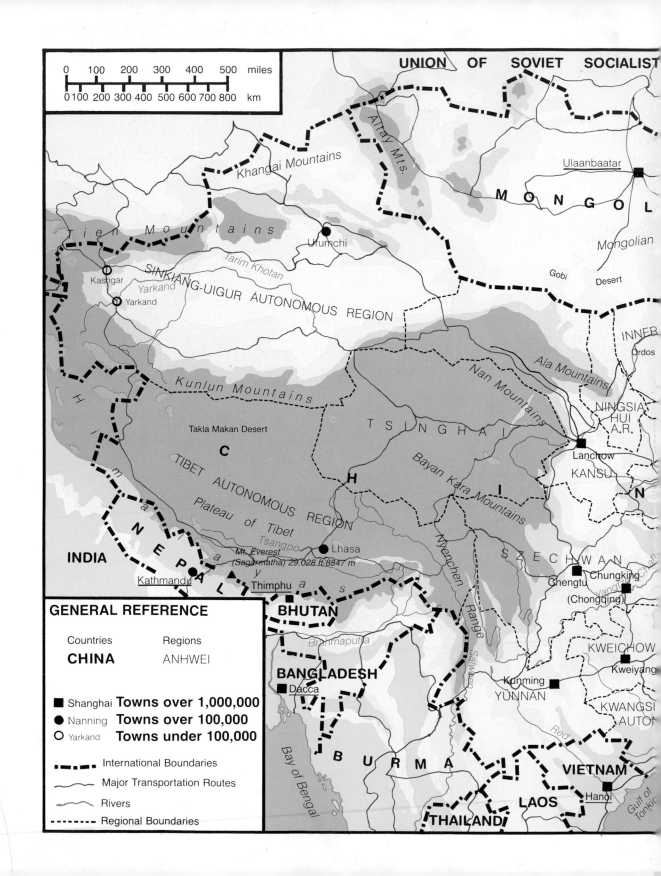

UNION OF SOVIET SOCIALIST

Khangai Mountains

Altay Mts.

Ulaanbaatar

M O N G O L

Mongolian

Tien Mountains

Tarim Khotan

Urumchi

Gobi   Desert

INNER

Kashgar

Yarkand

SINKIANG-UIGUR AUTONOMOUS REGION

Ordos

Ala Mountains

Nan Mountains

NINGSIA HUI A.R.

Kunlun Mountains

H
I

Takla Makan Desert

T S I N G H A I

Bayan Kara Mountains

Lanchow

KANSU

N

C

TIBET AUTONOMOUS REGION

H

I

Plateau of Tibet

Tsangpo

Nyenchen

S Z E C H W A N

Mt. Everest
(Sagarmatha) 29,028 ft 8847 m
y
Thimphu

Lhasa

Range

Chengtu
(Chongqing)

Chungking

Kathmandu

N E P A L

a s

INDIA

BHUTAN

Brahmaputra

BANGLADESH

Dacca

KWEICHOW

Kweiyang

Kunming
YUNNAN

KWANGSI
AUTON

B U R M A

Red

VIETNAM

Bay of Bengal

LAOS

Hanoi

Gulf of Tonkin

THAILAND

GENERAL REFERENCE

Countries	Regions
CHINA	ANHWEI

■ Shanghai **Towns over 1,000,000**

● Nanning **Towns over 100,000**

○ Yarkand **Towns under 100,000**

▬ ▬ International Boundaries

─── Major Transportation Routes

~~~ Rivers

- - - Regional Boundaries

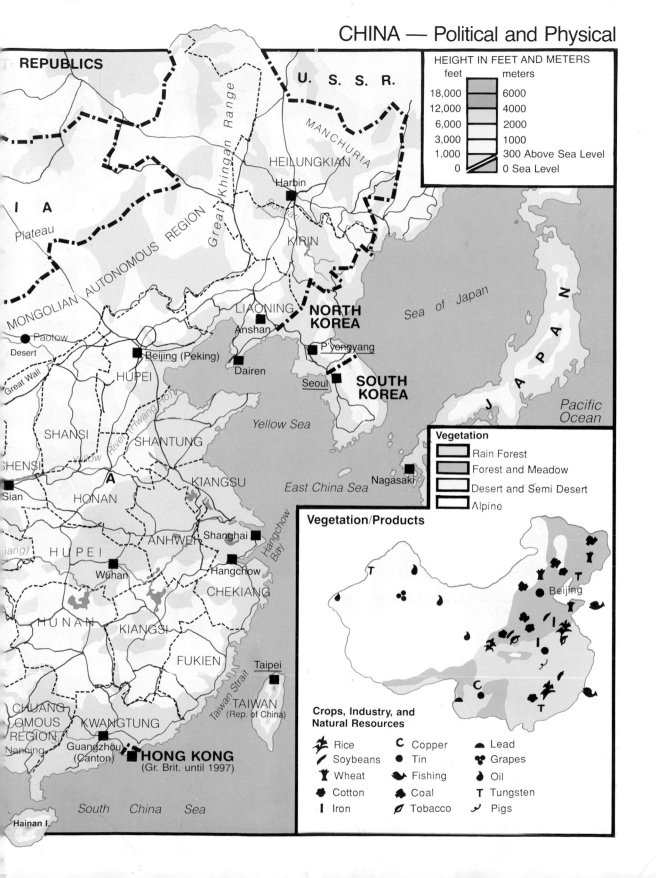

CHINA — Political and Physical

REPUBLICS

U. S. S. R.

HEIGHT IN FEET AND METERS

feet	meters	
18,000	6000	
12,000	4000	
6,000	2000	
3,000	1000	
1,000	300	Above Sea Level
0	0	Sea Level

MANCHURIA

HEILUNGKIAN

Harbin

Sungari

Great Khingan Range

KIRIN

MONGOLIAN AUTONOMOUS REGION

Plateau

I A

Paotow

Desert

LIAONING

Anshan

NORTH KOREA

P'yongyang

Sea of Japan

Beijing (Peking)

Dairen

Great Wall

HUPEI

Seoul

SOUTH KOREA

J A P A N

Pacific Ocean

SHANSI

SHANTUNG

River (Hwang Ho)

Yellow

Yellow Sea

SHENSI

A

KIANGSU

East China Sea

Nagasaki

Sian

HONAN

Vegetation

Rain Forest

Forest and Meadow

Desert and Semi Desert

Alpine

iang)

H U P E I

Wuhan

ANHWEI

Shanghai

Hangchow

Hangchow Bay

Vegetation/Products

CHEKIANG

H U N A N

KIANGSI

Beijing

FUKIEN

Taipei

TAIWAN (Rep. of China)

Taiwan Strait

CHUANG OMOUS REGION

Nanning

KWANGTUNG

Guangzhou (Canton)

HONG KONG (Gr. Brit. until 1997)

C

T

Crops, Industry, and Natural Resources

South China Sea

Hainan I.

🌾	Rice	C	Copper	◣	Lead
⟋	Soybeans	●	Tin	❦	Grapes
⊥	Wheat	🐟	Fishing	◖	Oil
❦	Cotton	❀	Coal	T	Tungsten
I	Iron	⌀	Tobacco	∿	Pigs

Education

Confucius thought education should teach people to be wise and good. In the past, Chinese who wanted government jobs had to show that they could read and write and also that they knew Confucius' teachings.

In 1949, just after the revolution, only 20% of the population could read. Today nearly 75% can read. Chinese schools stress science and technology to improve the standard of living. Moral education is still important, but now the emphasis is on teaching socialist goals and values.

Preschool Education

Children from three to six attend kindergarten. The children learn correct speech, simple arithmetic, moral values, art, and music. Children under three attend nurseries. Medical staffs check on the health of preschool children.

Elementary Schools

About 95% of China's children attend elementary school. City children attend better than country children do, but the government tries to bring education to rural children. It uses traveling teachers and sometimes even mobile schools.

Chinese children start elementary school when they are six or seven and stay for five years. In school they study the Chinese language, math, science, music, painting, and politics. In 3rd grade, they begin English, Russian, or another foreign language. In the upper grades they also do some manual work to teach them to respect labor.

Secondary School

In the cities most secondary-school students go to school for five years. Most rural students attend for three years. Besides continuing the subjects they studied in elementary school, students study history, hygiene, literature, and physiology. They are in school for seven hours a day, six days a week.

Students work a few hours each week in the small factories or workshops that are part of secondary schools. They make simple objects like radio parts. Not all students can go on to universities or technical colleges, so vocational schools often train students who are near the end of secondary school.

Universities and Technical Colleges

To enter a university or technical college students must pass exams, including one that tests their loyalty to the Communist Party. They must also do manual labor during the summer in order to remain in school. There are not enough schools or instructors for the large number of qualified students. Education is free. Thousands of Chinese study in other countries every year, and many foreign students study in China now.

University programs emphasize science and technology. Technical colleges train students in areas such as agriculture, forestry, medicine, mining, and teacher training.

People who do not pass entrance exams for universities and technical colleges can attend "workers' universities" at the factories where they work or they can take television or correspondence courses.

Sports

In recent years the Chinese have taken international medals in table tennis, badminton, volleyball, track and field, swimming, diving, and gymnastics. The government promotes and controls sports. It encourages physical exercise. In the big cities, it has built large stadiums and swimming pools. Factories must give employees two periods of 10-20 minutes for exercise every day. Many Chinese do *t'ai chi*, slow and graceful exercises that emphasize balance, relaxation, and correct breathing.

Beijing

About nine million people live in Beijing, a 3,000-year-old city, divided centuries ago into two parts: the northern Inner City and the southern Outer City. It has been the capital since the rule of Kublai Khan in the late 1200s. Inside the Inner City is the Imperial City, surrounded by a high red wall. Inside the Imperial City is the Forbidden City, once open only to the emperor and his court. In this city are manmade lakes and beautiful old palaces and temples. Today the cities are open to sightseers.

At one end of the Forbidden City is Tien An Men Square, a huge open area used for parades and political rallies. In the middle of the square is Mao Zedong Memorial Hall, containing Mao's tomb. Nearby is the great Hall of the People, where the National People's Congress and other government bodies meet.

Imperial dishes (clockwise from top): crab, egg, and tomato; onion cake; chicken and green pepper; fried duck; peanuts. Center: jellyfish salad with green preserved eggs.

Two hours north of Beijing by bus or car are portions of the Great Wall, called the "Long Wall of Ten Thousand Li" by the Chinese. Workers began it in the 5th century BC and finished it in 221 BC. It is the largest manmade structure on Earth, the only manmade structure astronauts see when they circle the Earth. Near the wall are Ming dynasty tombs where archeologists have found treasures from the past.

People travel in Beijing by subway or bus, bicycle, taxi, or pedicab, which is a three-wheeled bicycle cab. There are some official cars but no private cars, so Beijing does not have the traffic jams and auto fumes of many large cities.

Besides the palaces, temples, and government buildings, there are museums, hotels, restaurants, libraries, schools, and universities in Beijing. Streets are lined with old houses and newer apartment buildings, shops, and offices. The government still needs more houses for the people. Beijing is becoming a modern city.

Taiwan

Taiwan, an island about 100 miles (161 km) off the southeast coast of China, was governed as part of China from the late 1600s until the Japanese took control after defeating the Chinese in a war in 1895. Japan gave up Taiwan in 1945, after its defeat in World War II. In 1949, the Chinese Nationalists, under Chiang Kai-shek, fled to Taiwan after their defeat by the communists and set up their own one-party government on the island. All that was left of the Republic of China could now be found on Taiwan.

For many years Western governments opposed the communist regime in mainland China. Some, like the US, supported the Nationalists on Taiwan with money, military advisors, and weapons. In 1979, the US recognized the Beijing government as the actual government of China and later withdrew from its defense treaty with Taiwan. Today leaders of the People's Republic are trying to persuade the Taiwan government to become part of China again. So far, Taiwan is not interested in doing so. Its governor, Chiang Ching-kuo, Chiang Kai-Shek's son, has recently freed people from prison who disagreed with the Nationalist party, and other political parties are appearing on Taiwan. But communist parties are still not allowed, and many personal restrictions still exist.

Chinese in North America

Some scholars believe that people from China came across the Pacific and settled in North and South America around 2500 BC. These Chinese might be the ancestors of Native Americans.

The earliest *known* Chinese to arrive in North America came to California in the late 1840s gold rush. In the 1860s many were hired at low wages on construction of the first intercontinental railroad. After the railroad was built, they could not find work because Americans would not hire them. This was difficult for these men who had left their families in China, hoping to return to them richer.

The US then passed laws which kept new Chinese workers and even the families of present workers out of the US. Many US residents treated Chinese already in the US badly. For protection, the Chinese began living together in Chinatowns in big cities like San Francisco, Los Angeles, and New York.

After World War II, Americans became ashamed of the way they had treated the Chinese. They got rid of the ban on Chinese immigration. Many families were reunited. Many of the Chinese entering the US today are professionals like doctors, teachers, or engineers. Many Chinese in North America generally are here as university students and will return to China.

Many more Chinese are visiting North America now than in the past. This increase reflects the growing freedom the Chinese have to travel. The number of Chinese coming to North America to live permanently has also increased. In 1977 only 798 immigrated to Canada, while 6,550 did so in 1981. The numbers dropped after 1982 when Canada limited immigration because of economic problems. It has continued to drop since. The Chinese have moved to the US in more steady numbers. In 1976, about 23,000 moved to the US, while 25,000 did so in 1986.

More Books About China

Here are more books about China. If you are interested in them, check your library. They may be useful in doing research for the following "Things to Do."

Chinese Americans. Meltzer (Crowell)
Great Wall of China. Fisher (Macmillan)
Holding Up the Sky: Young People in China. Rau (Lodestar Books)
Magic Boat and Other Chinese Folk Stories. Jagendorf (Vanguard)
Minority Peoples of China. Rau (Messner)
Modern China. Carter (Franklin Watts)
Once There Were No Pandas: A Chinese Legend. Greaves (Dutton)

Glossary of Useful Chinese Terms (in Pinyin spelling)

baotzu (BOW-tzoo) . . . . dough wrapped around a filling and fried or steamed
hen hao (hern-HOW) . . . . . . very good
mantoh (MAHN-toh) . . . . bread
ni hao (nee-HOW) . . . . hello
xie xie (shiay-shiay) . . . . thank you
youyi (yo-YEE) . . . . friendship
zaijian (dzy-JEN) . . . . goodbye

Things to Do — Research Projects

For many years, the Chinese people have not had much contact with people outside China's borders. Now the government wants to trade more often with non-Chinese countries. This means many more foreigners will be visiting China on business and as tourists, and other countries will be seeing more Chinese visitors. As you read about developments in China, keep in mind the importance of current facts. Some of the research projects that follow need accurate, up-to-date information from current sources. Two publications that your library may have will tell you about recent newspaper and magazine articles on many topics:

Readers' Guide to Periodical Literature
Children's Magazine Guide

For a clear understanding of such topics as how China is changing its policies toward other nations, look up *China*. Then look under that for more specific topics like *Trade, Imports,* and *Exports.* They will lead you to the most up-to-date information from current sources.

1. About 55 minority nationalities living in China do not strictly obey rules set down by the Communist Party. These people, who live in isolated areas, follow some of their own traditions. Check encyclopedias to see what a tribe's life might be like. The names of some tribes are the Yao, Miao, Hui, Mongols, Tibetans, Uygurs, Kazakhs, Kirghiz, Zhuang, Yi (Lolo), and Manchu.

2. Think of an occupation or career that interests you. Would you be able to do this kind of work in China? Would being male or female make a difference?

3. Try to find out more about the cause of the Opium Wars. The company that apparently caused all the trouble was the British East India Company.

More Things to Do — Activities

These projects will give you a chance to think more about China. They offer ideas for interesting group or individual projects for school or home.

1. Calligraphy, or brush writing, is as much an art in China as painting. Find books on calligraphy in your library and study the characters and the ideas they stand for. Try to write some characters yourself.

2. Visit a shopping mall or department store. Look at the labels of toys, clothing, and other products. What can you find that was made in China?

3. For a pen pal in the People's Republic of China, write to these people:

International Pen Friends
P.O. Box 290065
Brooklyn, NY 11229-0001

Be sure to tell them what country you want your pen pal to be from. Also, include your full name and address.

Index